Guppy Primer
Ruth McIlroy

smith|doorstop

Published 2017 by
smith|doorstop books
The Poetry Business
Bank Street Arts
32–40 Bank Street
Sheffield S1 2DS

Copyright © Ruth McIlroy 2017
All Rights Reserved

ISBN 978-1-910367-80-3
Typeset by Utter
Printed by People for Print, Sheffield

Acknowledgements
Thanks are due to *Brittle Star*, *Chapman*, The Philip Larkin/East Riding Prize, Stramullion Publishing, *The Next Review*, *The Rialto*, Templar, Ver Poets and York Literature Festival.

smith|doorstop books are a member of Inpress: www.inpressbooks.co.uk. Distributed by NBN International, Airport Business Centre, 10 Thornbury Road Plymouth PL 6 7PP

The Poetry Business gratefully acknowledges the support of Arts Council England.

Contents

3	I am not Honest
4	Will you be my Bridesmaid
5	Just Idiot Talk
6	Getting a Start in Farming
7	Guppy Primer
9	Giordano Bruno
10	Incantation I (From the Scottish Gaelic)
11	Incantation II
12	Incantation III
13	One-Trick Pony
15	Stance
16	The Way of Strategy
17	Gaps
18	Injunctions to the Hesitant
19	DSM IV
21	Dornbusch
22	The Judas Song
23	Durst
24	All That
25	Fionnphort Crossing
26	Spider Brain Tally
27	Settle
28	Old Man with Cane and Panama
29	Around/In
30	Song of the Pauper
31	Out of the Woods
32	after a dream

For Tom and Sam

I am not Honest

I am not honest.

My heart is a walnut;
I know nothing.

I enjoy dozens of exotic holidays a year.
I'm a girl but I've just always loved a scrap.

Anyway.

I do not suffer fools;
I suffer larks.
I suffer a peck of Dull Rubbish.

I am nothing
if not.

I believe myself to have become a little brutal.
£904 is paid every month into my bank account.

I do not know how to pronounce Eurydice.

Will you be my Bridesmaid

think happy thoughts!
because you are best over the other ones ha ha

making the world a more cheerful place
one colourful accessory at a time

shall we call the bestest man 'waspish'
or 'of a certain age',
let's maybe also call him 'formidable'
ha ha

don't be dull
join your random load of bollocks with mine
our girlish secrets

and if you are unwilling
I will leave you alone at a different table
and I will laugh with my mates
and you will have no mates

you are
the jewel
in my

Just Idiot Talk

"Hey, Sassenach! Ye gie me the boak,
Yir patter stinks; youse'll get it noo,
Ye cannae say a'thing, ya muckle-face numpty".

But, ya wee keelie, I'll jist dae it efter.
Missed yersel' there now, eh no, hen?
Ken, this's barry, nae tother a ball.

Glossary

Just Idiot Talk	Just an idiolect consciously employed to gain acceptance from a dominant social group
Hey, Sassenach	Excuse me, English person
ye gie me the boak	you make me feel nauseous
Yir patter stinks	your way of presenting yourself to the world is fundamentally flawed
youse'll get it noo	you (singular or plural) are about to experience retribution
Ye cannae say a'thing	I would advise you not to answer me back
ya muckle-face numpty	you ill-favoured person of limited common sense
But, ya wee keelie	But, you young person from a challenging home environment
I'll jist dae it efter	I'll just do it later
Missed yersel' there now	you didn't see that one coming
eh no, hen?	did you, my friend/acquaintance
Ken, this's barry	You know something, I feel a lot better
nae tother a ball	no bother at all

Getting a Start in Farming

anyone would think it would be nigh-on impossible to set up farming round here
well they'd be wrong

here's my pigs, a lovely fatty breed
they have to be crossed with a more modern breed

if you want to get the size
and you want to get the sausages out

only the bigger animals have sausages inside them when you open them up
these guys will go orf down to a local abattoir and then they will return

and we sell pork, lamb and beef in chunks
so we sell either a quarter of or half of a pig *oink oink*

we label them, we allocate them to all the different
then we deliver them on Wednesday

I take a white van, that van
I wear my white coat and my hat

and my white wellies and orf I go
and I go to Bristol and Bath and then up to London

there were twenty six cows and twenty six sheep
we hardly knew the difference when we began
we also sell live heifers surplus to our requirements
all of the animals going round all of the fields one after the other.

Guppy Primer

I

Beautiful Guppies don't just happen.
The secret is *sweat*, and attention to detail.
Treat them to good live food when you pass them from the left,
And siphon off 10% of their water when you pass them from the right.
Replace the water with aged good water, such as Bronx, NY
Tap water, which has a pH of 6.8.

Be sure to throw away the bad males, and before long
You'll have a tank of beautiful Guppies.

Learn to watch out for unscrupulous dealers
Who sell fancy males with common females.
Look out for babies hiding among the plants.
Guppies drop babies every 28 days or so.
Put them immediately in the breeding trap you bought
In anticipation of the Blessed Event.

(The best reason for providing a breeding trap is illustrated
By this photograph showing a female Guppy eating her young.)

Your purpose here is to end up with some virgin females;
Try to keep your babies sorted out according to sex.
Some of the females can go back in with their parents
To breed with their father or uncle, or be crossed
With their brothers in separate miniature jars.
Keep inbreeding your fish for a few generations;
This is the way new varieties spring up.

Breed those fish you like the best
With the virgin females.

But check the virgins first.

   II

I have seen the same Guppy sold
By four different people under four different names.
Hahnel's red Guppies, for example;

Flamingo Guppies; Flame Guppies;
Redtail Guppies; Fire Guppies;
Red Ruby Guppies; Whore Guppies;
Leopard Guppies; Green Guppies;
Swordtail Guppies; Veiltail Guppies;
English Golden Lacetail Guppies.

Beautiful Guppies don't just happen.

Giordano Bruno
From 'De la Causa, Principio e uno' (1584)

Cavallier of the order of the Most Christian King,
conseglier of his private Conseglio, captain of 50 men,
and ambassador to the Queen of England Serenissima,
reviled by knaves and persecuted by genii bestial, loved by savii,
admirato by scholars, magnified by large,
estimated to be powerful and favored by the gods;
I, for this much favor from you already ricettato
nodrito, defended, delivered, felt safe, kept in port,
escaped to you from perilous and mighty storm, consecrate to you
this anchor, these seamstresses, these fiaccate sails.

If all forms are contained as from that, and the same by virtue
produced and parturite; and who have not less than
raggione attualitànell'essere sensitive and explicit,
though not according to accidental existence,
being that everything you see open for accidents based on the size,
it is pure accident; remaining still the Substance detects and identifies
coincident with the matter. Waves, it is quite clear
that dall'esplicazione we can not take anything but damn,
the fate that sustanziali differences are occolte,
said Aristotle forced from the truth.

Incantation I (From the Scottish Gaelic)

Haar; bride out
Early morning
Horse with a friend
Horse broke his leg.
With much ado
That was apart
She put backbone to backbone
She put flesh to flesh
She put gullet to gullet
She put vein to vein.
As she is healing
I have this healing.

Incantation II

Rose death-like, deadly, swollen,
Leave the udder of the cow,
Leave the udder of the cat-heads,
Leave, leave that to single peat
And cross to single peat not you.

A stubborn rose, thrawn,
When cow udder,
Leave the pastry and the udder,
Flee to stone.

I place rose with stone,
I place stone to the stone floor,
I place milk in the udder,
I place substance in the kidney.

Incantation III

Third on the lawn of aesthetic,
The third is great dirty sea,
She herself is the best instrument to carry it,
  A great sea dirty,
  A great salt sea.

The name of the Tri Dull,
The name of the Tri Numh,
The name of Nan Uile Run,
The name of the Great Powers.

She herself is the best instrument to carry it,
  A great sea dirty,
  A great salt sea,
The best instrument to carry it.

Acknowledgements to A Carmichael, Carmina Gadelica II, Edinburgh (1900)

One-Trick Pony

you a one-trick pony
hoof me once too many
me out of here

oh, did love you
had your back
you never had mine

did good for you
but you kick up stour
frisky one thing   but was more

have to crash up, chuck and stir
clods and mud and rubble shower

me the one end up in mire

I'm not let you mucky me

have your head

there
I free

you go
I win, you know

dont want to

better if
we warm in stable
tar you hoof
comb you mane you muzzle

Stance
From Musashi's Book of Five Rings

Adopt a stance with the head erect,
Neither hanging down, nor looking up, nor twisted.
Your forehead and the space between your eyes

Should not be wrinkled. Do not roll your eyes
Nor allow them to blink, but slightly narrow them.
Keep the line of your nose straight, slightly flaring your nostrils.

Hold the line of the rear of the neck
Straight. Instil vigour into your hairline.
Lower both shoulders, put strength in your legs

From the knees to the tips of your toes.
Make the everyday stance your combat stance.
The gaze should be large and broad.

It is important to know the enemy's sword
And not be distracted by insignificant movements.
When you cannot be deceived by men

You will have realised the wisdom of strategy.
Your spirit should be settled, yet unbiased;
Do not let the enemy see your spirit.

The Way of Strategy
From Musashi's Book of Five Rings

When I reached thirty, I looked back on my past.
My victories had little to do with strategy;
More to the order of heaven perhaps; or natural ability,

Or the others' inferior strategy. I resolved
To master strategy, and studied morning and night.
I came to the Way of Strategy when I was fifty.

Since then I have lived without following any particular Way.
Thus, with the virtue of strategy, I practice
Many arts and abilities – all with no teacher.

If you want to learn of this Way, consider these things
One at a time; you must do sufficient research.
I cannot write in detail how this is done.

To write this poem I did not use the law of Buddha,
Or the teachings of Confucius. It is the night of the tenth day
Of the tenth month, at the hour of the tiger.

Gaps
(to the tune of Streets of Laredo)

One night, at a lighthouse, I crept out to star-gaze;
I didn't remember the circling beam.
I sat on the bench and looked up at the heavens.
(Constellations – then nothing – constellations – the beam).

As I felt my way back by the curve of the sea-wall
It was,   , stars,   ,stars,   , stars,   ;
And to fill in the gaps then my brain took a fancy
(There was dream   not dream, beam   not beam, dream   not dream, beam).

It pulled out some scraps of old song-lines and sayings
On the tip of my tongue; yes, like that, no, not that.
And I watched them come streaming, my dear higher functions,
Stuttering on in the dark; let them run, let them run.

Injunctions to the Hesitant

Get ready. Get steady. Then go.
Start when you're ready,
go when you're steady,
and never repeat; and don't miss a beat,
gather ye rosebuds while you may,
don't tarry along that road. Sweet day!

So cool, so calm, so bright; but stop;
to plagiarise is not an option
in the place you've landed up,
this kingdom of the half-filled cup –

glorious, glorious cup half-full,
go tell it to the mountain, rule
the dum-de-dumming of this land
and and and and, and and and – and

DSM IV
(The DSM IV Diagnostic Manual classes Personality Disorders under Axis II)

Personality
Listenaropy
Personlaity
Stripyalone
Aye nor split.

I am called to a field of beneficence,
a field multi-axial, across five dimensions.
If I am to be haltlose, haughty, histrionic,
prithee then, let me be Axis II.

I dwell in a field of beneficence,
Deploying chameleon-like social skills.
There's many a notion in public works
specifically meant for me.

Praise me! PRAISE ME! **P**rovocative **R**elationships
Attention **I**nfluenced **S**peech **E**motional
Makeup **E**xaggerated. (I do I do this?)
(Numerous other strategies are used.)

I am placed in a field of beneficence,
an environment experienced as invalidating.
Mercurial disorder; I dwell on the border,
Oh folie maniaco; oh, folie! said he.

He's a loosely-conceived designation,
Experiencing disregulation,
Amygdalaic activation,

And melancholique ideation,
And overly passionate notions,
And slowly-subsiding emotions.

I am called to a field of beneficence.
And I am greatly loved.
And I am deeply grateful for my life.

Listen! A ropy
Person: laity?
Stripy, alone –

Aye, nor split.

Dornbusch

DORNBUSCH was founded in 1900;
the manufacture of Machinery such as Embossing Calendars
and Multi Color Printing Machines for the Textile
and Artificial Leather Industry was introduced.

The DORNBUSCH name then became internationally
recognised as a versatile company.
In 1971 it was decided to exclude
of the machine division allowing DORNBUSCH

to revert to its particular force – the creation
and production of: Embossing Rollers, Embossing Plates, Printing Rollers.
DORNBUSCH has a very well-earned world-wide reputation
based on the first class products, excellent service

and competitive pricing. DORNBUSCH became
a major player in evidence at all
the important world fairs, and in 2009
a poet arrived – WELCOME TO DORNBUSCH!

The Judas Song

Richard Strauss, who served under Hitler,
'warmed to him', and returned to form.
Here's to traitors; let's hear it for turncoats,
doing their stuff while the principled burn.

Give me a Stasi, a weak double-crosser;
oh I'm a one for collaborators, me.
There, by the grace of god – yes, *by*, you rhymesters,
pariahs, and two-faced informers – go we.

Durst

There it is, you're caught.
You're right, of course.
But you can't imagine.

Arrest him.
I don't know what's in the house.
I'm having difficulty with the question.

He was right, I was wrong.
And the bumping.

Oh, I want this. What a disaster.
What the hell did I do? Killed them all of course.

All That

He made some big mistakes; he sold the sandwich bar
the year before the office blocks began to open.
The neighbourhood had been re-zoned commercial; he must have heard.

Back on the airport taxis, he'd invent life-stories
until one day a passenger said 'We were in your cab last week'.
After that he grew a big fat stomach, putting it down to boredom.

The man's life was full of holes. Sweet basil grew along his windowsill,
garlic from the Halal store, his table spread with onions,
plum tomatoes, parmagiana, olive oil from Lucca.

'You know what would pay round here,' he'd say, 'dog-walking.
'Walking people's dogs for money. But will he listen?
'Useless, that boy of ours, no effing use at all.'

Fionnphort Crossing

Iain MacGillivray, the captain and owner
of Pride of the Hebrides, a one-car ferry
(the pride consisting of taking her out
whatever the weather, between Fionnphort and Iona),

talked of the four young lads going home
over the same strait only last summer
using their own sturdy boat, but had taken a few,
and just the one made it, he said, and so on;

so when you clung on, and clamped your eyes shut,
and begged me to say the waves had got smaller,
in that rusty old skip, excuse for a ferry,
and the mountainous seas over us on both sides,

and I said we were safe, and I lied, and I lied,
and you later proclaimed I'd stepped up to the mark,
well, it wasn't like that; for you still do not know
of the deep laugh that swelled up, that swelled up inside.

Spider Brain Tally

I left a kilo of squirrel in the gutter

but what about the bucket of spiders I've saved this year –
will one or any of them step up or stand by me?

thirty forty spider brains twinking in my garden
all because of me, my rescue spiders

not to mention all the other
little animal centres
who will map or audit the prickle of brains, bee, aphid,
brown ant, beetle, teeming unseen, outside?

now, when I walk
I walk this brainscape
step on a brain
we swallow brains
even vegans
even Jains!

I need to be clean and spare to write of spiders and their distribution.
Their livingness submerges me.
I cannot bear their mass or their corporeality.

I have appointed myself Chief Counter of the Brains
Citizen Spider Mrs Aphid
Dame Ant.

Settle

settle the poem it is not going anywhere
the moon is a harvest moon and therefore or also red

the moon is out of reach being outside, whereas inside one can settle

inside the capacious house I settled
paid obeisance to my footfall around the planks look   look
at the path taken between my door and my table

taken up space

albeit extraneous factors arise   that is
outside, a horseman and his gallant nag 'ride towards Death'

ah duende

why does the man go forward
why does he not settle?

give up little horseman it is better to hunker
the little black pony needs to be settled

settle the pony, it is not going anywhere
stable warm coat muzzle.

Old Man with Cane and Panama
for P.K.M 1930-2010

I was shoulder deep in the sea at Coney Island
when I saw you stepping down the beach,
singular and content.

I love to see you unencumbered.
You knew me from the others in the sea;
your steady look said 'What is this to me?'

I remembered winter; how we closed your eyes.
I thought that you were gone forever.
And now I hope, with a child's unreason.

Stay; don't stay, dear father; hold me
longer in your enigmatic gaze,
mild, unbending, in the Southern Brooklyn haze.

You turned and walked back up the beach;
the ocean held my arms down by my sides,
rocking me in the long Atlantic swell.

The jets roared over towards Newark, or JFK.

Around/In

when I walk in town
I am along with my fingernails

my hair rides too   above and behind me
so   apart from clothes
it is just two keys
which are not integral
but always come too

one makes my car go
it is the magical doorway to me going around
like a person with superpowers I go from here to over there

the other lets me in to safety when I have done with going around

without the metal I could be out   but not going around
caught out   stock   still   stark   naked   in the open

when I am still, I wish to be *in*
as there, naturally, I cannot be got

when I am not in   I head for this and for that
metal ably in service.

Song of the Pauper

Into your hands, O Lord, I commend my spirit.
Hide me under the shadow of your wings;
forgive me my necessary budgetings.

For we are the bones, broken and scattered, are we not,
lying cheerfully and stumpily around,
clattering quietly at each other's processes,
peace settling on us, against all reason.

Out of the Woods

I wish I were
coherent more

this year I am
clear of   bare

the moon is bare
Girl, that were

a right big moon. Staring you were

was already
half-way there

after a dream

in which I was getting caught out leaving something innocuous
                                        in a strange woman's house
I woke up with a German accent
and it had snown.